E. Cora Hind

Carlotta Hacker

Fitzhenry & Whiteside

Contents

THE CANADIANS®
A Continuing Series

E. Cora Hind
Author: Carlotta Hacker
Cover Illustration: John Mardon
Design: Kerry Designs
THE CANADIANS® *is a registered trademark of Fitzhenry & Whiteside Limited.*

Fitzhenry & Whiteside acknowledge with thanks the Canada Council for the Arts, the Government of Canada through its Book Publishing Industry Development Program, and the Ontario Arts Council for their support of our publishing program.
National Library of Canada Cataloguing in Publication
Hacker, Carlotta, 1931-
E. Cora Hind / Carlotta Hacker. -- Rev. ed.
(The Canadians)
Includes index.
ISBN 1-55041-834-3
1. Hind, E. Cora (Ella Cora), 1861-1942--Juvenile literature.
2. Journalists--Canada--Biography. 3. Feminists--Canada--Biography--Juvenile literature. I. Title. II. Series: Canadians
PN4913.H5H27 2003   j070.92   C2003-903424-0

Chapter 1
Canada's Most Famous Woman

"Wat's that woman doing in the show ring?" asked a scandalized spectator at an agricultural fair.

"That's no woman," came the half-joking reply. "That's E. Cora Hind."

In the early decades of this century, a familiar—if unusual—figure at fairs and cattle shows throughout western Canada was E. Cora Hind, a slight, matter-of-fact woman, dressed in riding breeches, a pair of serviceable boots and a fringed buckskin jacket. She boldly wore this outfit, even though trousers were considered unladylike in those days. She moved confidently among the judges, even though women were not allowed in the ring. She chatted with weather-beaten stockmen and cracked jokes with grizzled farmhands. Well-to-do ranchers doffed their Stetsons to her. Small-time sheep farmers greeted her as an old friend. In that very masculine assembly, everyone seemed to want to say hello or show livestock to her or ask her advice. For E. Cora Hind was not only the agricultural and commercial editor of the *Manitoba Free Press*, she was one of Canada's leading authorities on farming and marketing.

One of the many remarkable things about Cora Hind was that even the most macho cattlemen took it for granted that

E. Cora Hind in her famous costume

she should have a place of honour at their meetings and exhibitions. They tended to forget she was a member of the so-called "weaker sex." She had proved herself so capable and so knowledgeable about farming that they looked on her as a highly respected colleague, one of themselves. This, in spite of the fact that when she was not tramping through mud or scaling fences, she dressed as correctly as any other woman of her day and might even spend an evening baking gingerbread.

E. Cora Hind was very much aware that she was a woman. Born in the Victorian era, her rise to success had been slow and hard, simply because she was female.

Even after she had gained such fame that she was spoken of admiringly as "the best newspaper man in western Canada," she lacked many male privileges—such as the right to vote. She was a dedicated member of the suffrage movement, and all her life she spoke out strongly against any injustices suffered by women.

Her remarks were always to the point. Once, when she was complaining that girls were seldom allowed to lead in the foals or calves at exhibitions (because it was "unfeminine" to do so), she commented wryly: "Incidentally, it seems to have grown more unfeminine since the girls have developed a habit of taking championships." She was quick to note any hypocrisy. Flattery had no effect on her either. A British reporter, who suggested that she was "the grand old lady of Canadian journalism," was given a curt response. "Don't call me a lady," said Cora Hind brusquely. "Call me a woman. I may or may not be a lady, but I know I am a woman."

As a matter of fact, she was very much the lady. She had a strong sense of form, and she believed in doing the "proper" thing. But she did not believe in slavishly following a fashion or custom simply because everyone else was doing so. "Standardizing men and women leads as a rule to appalling mediocrity," she once said. A rugged individualist, she had the courage to be different when she thought being different was right—or merely sensible.

She used to take her knitting to press conferences and would sit there doing two plain, two purl, while reporters for rival papers were busily writing in their notebooks. She saw no reason why she should not knit. It did not prevent her from listening attentively or making notes when necessary. Similarly, although an active member of the Women's Christian Temperance Union, she saw no reason why, on one occasion, she should not drink a toast with a glass of wine. It was the polite thing to do in the circumstances. Cora Hind always kept her sense of proportion— and her sense of humour. Having let wine pass her lips, she wrote and told her WCTU friends that she had liked the taste.

E. Cora Hind in her office at the Free Press *in the 1930s*

Nobody could ever accuse Cora Hind of lacking common sense. It was one of her dominant qualities. But perhaps determination was even more basic to her character: determination to speak out and say what needed to be said, even if it was unpopular; to do what she thought right, regardless of public opinion; to succeed at whatever she tackled; and, especially, to get her own way. This was evident even as a small child, when she decided that she did not like her first name, Ella. In the future, people would please call her by her second name, Cora. They did, and Ella was reduced to an initial.

And so it was that "E. Cora Hind" became known both nationally and internationally as an outstanding journalist, lecturer, writer and foremost authority on all aspects of agriculture. In the 1930s a European newspaper claimed that she was "Canada's most famous woman." It was a reputation she had achieved entirely through her own efforts—and in spite of an unpromising start in life.

Chapter 2
Go West, Young Woman

Cora Hind was orphaned in early childhood. Her mother died when she was two years old, her father, when she was five. She never really knew either of them, though she was greatly influenced by what she knew about them.

Her father's family had emigrated from the pottery district of Derbyshire, England, and settled as homesteaders near Toronto in the 1840s. Her father, Edwin Hind, became a stonemason, but he was as much an artist as a mason. He carved many of the figures that decorate St. James Cathedral in Montreal and Osgoode Hall in Toronto. There was talent on the maternal side too. James Carroll Hind, Cora's mother, had won a prize at the age of seventeen for writing the best essay in the city of Toronto. This was following a family tradition. Her uncle (Cora's great-uncle) was the Rev. John Carroll, author of several books on Methodism. One of his books, *The School of the Prophets*, was a bestseller among Methodists.

The Carrolls were descended from United Empire Loyalists who had settled in Nova Scotia and then moved to York County, so there were British allegiances on both sides of the family. These ties were fostered by Cora's grandfather, old Joseph Hind, who used to tell Cora stories of his childhood at Mugginton in Derbyshire. Time tends to soften memories, and Mugginton, in spite of its name, sounded like an idyllic village. As Cora grew up, she nurtured her love for the Old Country until, as a teenager, she found a rival suitor. Hearing Sir John A. Macdonald speak in Orillia, she realized that she was first and foremost a Canadian. "My country was swelling in my heart," she wrote. For the rest of her life she maintained a deep love for the land of her birth.

Cora was born in Toronto on September 18, 1861, her parents' third and last child. When her mother died two years later, Cora and her brothers, Joseph and George, were sent to

live with their grandfather, Joseph Hind, who had a farm at Artemesia in Grey County, Ontario. He took the children because their father was so often away from home doing masonry work. In fact Edwin Hind was in Chicago when he caught cholera and died in 1866.

Cora Hind grew up among Ontario homesteaders like these people

In spite of losing both parents in the first few years of her life, Cora seems to have had a happy childhood. Her aunt, Alice Hind, took over the role of mother. Joseph Hind acted as father as well as grandfather, and he also became Cora's counsellor and friend. Some of her happiest childhood hours were spent with her grandfather. He would take her round his farm, explaining how the wheat should be sown and tended, how to check its ripeness, how to look for the points of a horse—and always taking time to answer her eager questions.

The Hinds lived much like other homesteading families, making their own soap and candles, bottling preserves, sugaring off the maple syrup in the spring and relying on their livestock and the income from their wheat. An early frost could spell disaster, as it did one year. Cora knew what frozen wheat

By the time Cora Hind took her teacher's exams in 1882, schoolrooms with women teachers were common in Ontario

looked like long before she became a recognized authority on agriculture.

It was a hard year when the crop froze, but the Hinds struggled through like other homesteaders. They were fairly self-sufficient and did not have many expenses. Aunt Alice made most of the clothing, and at first it was she who taught the children their lessons. Cora did not begin school until she was eleven, for there was no school to go to. Then, in 1872, Spring Hill School was built on the corner of her grandfather's land, and Cora became one of the first students. Later, when her grandfather moved to Flesherton, Ontario, Cora attended the public school there. She completed her education at the high school in Orillia, staying with her uncle, George Hind. It was there, in 1882, that she wrote her third-class teacher's examination.

Cora was twenty years old by this time, a young woman from the country with a good basic education. It was almost inevitable that she should train to be a schoolmistress. Teaching was one of the few professions open to women, though nursing had also

Go West Young Woman

become respectable since Florence Nightingale's reforms in the 1850s. In addition, there were a few, very few, women doctors in Canada and a handful of women medical students. But 1882 was the year that Queen's University students went on strike to protest the presence of women medics. Though such opposition would not have deterred Cora, she had no desire to become a doctor. In any case, her family would have had a hard time finding the college fees.

Journalism, the career Cora favoured most, also posed financial problems. She was expected to bring in an immediate and regular income. She could not afford to sit at home writing articles in the hope that some of them might occasionally be published, and without connections she knew that she had no chance of getting on the staff of a newspaper or magazine. Only very rarely were women hired. As a rule, they could not even work in offices—clerks and secretaries were male.

Egerton Ryerson

Women could of course work as servants, and they could take labouring jobs on farms or in factories, especially in the garment industry. But the only profession that required them in large numbers was teaching. This was a fairly recent development. Although women had always run "dames' schools" and "establishments for young ladies," education had traditionally been considered a male preserve. It was Egerton Ryerson, as superintendent of education, who widened the field by advocating free schooling for all children so that the poor as well as the rich could receive an education. When this practice became law under the 1871 Ontario School Act, a great many teachers were suddenly needed. There were not enough men available to fill all the posts, so women were recruited. Cora planned to join their ranks, partly because there was no reasonable alternative and partly to please her Aunt Alice.

It was while she was waiting to hear the results of her teacher's examination that her cousins, Joseph and James Jacques, visited the Hind household. They had been out West and were seething with excitement about the opportunities there and the fortunes to be made. This was the era of the "opening up" of the West, when the Canadian Pacific Railway was being built, when settlers were moving out by the thousands to take up land, when new towns were springing up almost overnight and established towns were growing at an unbelievable rate. Winnipeg, for example, had doubled its population in a single year—from about 7,000 in 1881 to almost 14,000 in 1882. There was work for all, the Jacques brothers insisted.

Cora's Aunt Alice was the first to catch the enthusiasm. She was not needed in Flesherton any more. The Hind children were grown up. She decided to try her luck in the West. Cora immediately said she would go too. Her cousins assured her that teachers were required in Manitoba, but Cora felt that teaching was only one possibility. The West was a whole new world. Anything could happen there.

Cora and her aunt set off in high spirits, taking the boat from Collingwood to Duluth, then travelling by train through Minnesota, west to St. Paul and then north to Winnipeg. They arrived there in August 1882. They had been intending to push on to Brandon, but when they heard that it was still only a tent city, they decided to stay in Winnipeg, though Winnipeg itself was not quite what they had imagined.

Their first sight of the city must have been a surprise. The streets were certainly not paved with gold. They were not paved at all. Even the main thoroughfares were black earthen tracks, which turned into a quagmire of sticky mud the moment any rain fell. The mud clung to everything, to the wheels of the carts, to people's boots. It was tracked onto the raised boardwalks that lined the streets. On a wet day, the floors of stores and houses were soon carpeted with mud.

The whole city had a very messy appearance because of the recent building boom. In the past year, since Winnipeg had learned that it was to be on the mainline of the CPR, there had been a turmoil of activity. People were arriving from the East to set up stores and hotels, to help build them or simply to speculate in real estate. Land had been bought and sold at ever-rising prices, and houses were going up at a feverish rate. Some of them still had canvas roofs. Others were "tarpaper homes"—wooden shacks that looked like black-patched boxes because they had been covered with tarpaper to keep out the wind. The outskirts of town sprawled with tents and sheds of every description. Although for a whole year Winnipeg had been a land of promise, it certainly did not look like one.

From Main Street, the open prairies could be seen, stretching flat and featureless as far as the horizon. The city was still only a fraction of its present size. But as a result of the boom, some urban services had been provided. The telephone exchange had been in operation for more than a year. Mail delivery had been started in February 1882; and in August, just about the time of Cora's arrival, a streetcar service had come into operation, running along Broadway, Kennedy, Portage and Main. The streetcars were horse-drawn, and the rails were set on planks to keep the horses' feet out of the mud. Main Street would remain unpaved for two more years, and ten years would pass before

Main Street, Winnipeg, c. 1883. The sixth building from the left is the Davis House, where Cora Hind and her aunt spent their first night.

electric trolley cars rattled through Winnipeg. But in the meantime electric streetlights were being installed, using electricity generated at the Hudson's Bay Company gristmill on the Assiniboine River. Two months after Cora arrived, Winnipeg had its first electric lights—one at the CPR station, one at the corner of Broadway and three on Main.

Main Street, like a few others in the centre of town, already had a metropolitan appearance, although it was not as elegant as the drawings of the time led one to believe. But Main could boast some impressive three and even four-storey buildings that would not have looked out of place in Toronto or Montreal. It was definitely a city street with its banks and stores and hotels. Also on Main Street was a small two-storey building, the Davis House, where Cora and her aunt spent their first night.

After a few days at the Davis House, Alice Hind found rooms for herself and Cora in the Dundee Block on Main Street, and from there she advertised her services as a dressmaker. Dressmakers were needed, for there were not many people in the city who were prepared to do this kind of work. Most of the women were either wives of businessmen or prostitutes. A great many prostitutes had been attracted to Winnipeg because of the hundreds of men who had gone there to work on building sites or on the CPR. It was a wide-open frontier town that Cora and her aunt had come to.

Surprisingly, it was also a town on the verge of a depression. Too much had happened too quickly, and the boom was already beginning to collapse. Everyone had been too enthusiastic, and prices had been inflated out of all proportion. The Hinds arrived just when the reaction was beginning to set in. Speculators were losing fortunes as quickly as they had made them only a few months earlier. Wages were no longer high. A man who had earned $5 a day (a good salary at the time) now found he could get only $2. There was far less money in circulation. Cora had not been in Winnipeg a week before she realized that she was only going to make her way there by hard work.

She does not seem to have been dismayed, though she should have been appalled at her situation—travelling all that way at great expense, only to find that the golden land of opportunity was no more than a wind-swept, mud-caked straggle of a town where even jobs might be hard to find. On top of all this was the letter she received a few days after her arrival, a letter telling her that she had failed her teacher's exam.

Aunt Alice wanted her to study for it again, for she had only failed in one subject, algebra. But Cora had other ideas. Here in the West, she felt she might have a chance in journalism, for she had a good contact. W.F. Luxton, the editor of the *Manitoba Free Press*, was a friend of her uncle, George Hind, with whom she had stayed in Orillia. Uncle George had written her a letter of introduction.

Armed with this letter, Cora went to the newspaper offices. Luxton received her courteously, inquiring after George Hind and being thoroughly charming until he realized why Cora had come to visit him. Then he became patronizing. In a fatherly manner he explained that a newspaper office was no place for a young lady. It was a dirty place; there was oily machinery, printer's ink. Sometimes one had to work late hours. Sometimes one had to meet people who were not entirely respectable. He made it clear that he had no intention of employing Cora. Not only was she totally inexperienced, but he had no women on his staff and he did not intend to hire any.

Cora listened politely, but she was not impressed by Luxton's explanations. She knew that some women did work in journalism. She would not have wasted her time visiting him if she had thought it impossible to become a reporter. She knew that there were a number of newspaperwomen in the United States. There were even a few in Canada, working as sub-editors as well as writers. A managing editor had praised their work to C.S. Clark, the author of *Toronto the Good*, saying that as proofreaders, women did the work just as well as men. Not that this impressed Clark, who commented scathingly:

> As a matter of fact they do better than men, in some branches ... I assert that there is no one more competent to throw dirt than a woman ... Some eight years ago Grip had on its staff a cantankerous disappointed old harridan who used to write acidulated dirt which she thought was satire. I never saw her and do not know her name, yet the way she wrote of Prof. Goldwin Smith and Lord Randolph Churchill convinced me that I was correct. No one but a disappointed woman could have framed such language ...
> As long as the woman journalist confines herself to descriptions of sleeves and flounces and subjects equally inane, she will be all

The office of the Manitoba Free Press in 1883

right, but when it comes to a discussion of other subjects, she cannot discuss on their merits—she is sure to show her vindictive nature.

Clark had a very low opinion of women, whatever their calling. According to him, female intellectuals were spiteful muckrakers and the rest of the gender were lewd temptresses. But his statements represented quite a large body of opinion.

Cora had hoped that in the West things would be different. She had set great store by her uncle's letter. She was very disappointed, but she refused to be discouraged. Having seen the inside of a newspaper office and felt the bustle and excitement, she knew that this was the world in which she really wanted to work. She would not retake her teacher's exam, however much Aunt Alice wanted her to. She would find some other employment. And in the meantime she would write something for the paper.

A few months later she submitted an article to Luxton. To her surprise he accepted it, though he could not bring himself to credit her as the author. Rather than bring it out under a woman's name, he published it anonymously. But at least he published it.

Cora was jubilant. A story in the newspaper—and she was barely twenty-one years old! Fortunately, she did not know that nearly twenty more years would pass before she would be offered a job at the *Free Press*. Her road to success was to be uphill all the way.

Chapter 3
First Typist in the West

Looking back over the lives of the famous, it is all too easy to see only the success story. One forgets that most of these achievers were once ordinary teenagers or self-doubting young adults. Certainly they had dreams and ambitions, but they did not know whether their dreams would ever come true.

At the age of twenty-one, Cora's future must have looked very bleak, in spite of the one article that had been published. She had failed to become a teacher; she had failed to become a newspaperwoman; and she was in no position to devote her time to writing. She had to get a job and bring in some income. There were two obvious courses open to her. She could swallow her pride, forget her ambitions and try the teacher's exam again. Or she could give up all hopes of a career and help her aunt at dressmaking. She did not do either.

Calling on a Winnipeg lawyer to get a legal paper signed, she learned that a new line of work had become open to women in the United States. Women were actually working in offices, operating typewriting machines. It is doubtful if Cora had ever seen one of these machines. Although Remington had been marketing a commercial model since 1874, that machine only typed capital letters and was of no great practical use. But a shift-key model had been invented in 1878, and in the past few years it had become popular in the States. No firm in Winnipeg had one yet—writing was all done by hand—but a go-ahead businessman had recently opened an agency in the city hoping to sell a few machines. Cora visited him and rented one of his models for a month. If she could learn to type, she felt she might get a job in an office. Surely somebody in Winnipeg would be adventurous enough to employ her, in spite of her gender.

By the end of the month, she had taught herself to type—not very fast, to be sure, but at least she could operate the machine competently. When she returned it to the agency, the manager told her that he had made a sale the previous day to lawyers Macdonald and Tupper, though they had admitted that nobody on their staff knew how to use the machine. Cora went straight to their offices and applied for a job. She was interviewed by Hugh John Macdonald, the son of Sir John A. Macdonald, given a typing test and hired on the spot. Macdonald offered her a salary of $6 a week, which she considered good pay.

Nowadays it is no great news if a twenty-one-year-old woman gets a job as a typist, but in 1883 it was a breakthrough. Cora was entering the "men only" world. Furthermore, she was pioneering in technology. In later years she was always proud to claim that she had been the first typist in Canada west of the Great Lakes. Soon she was listing herself in the Winnipeg Street Directory as a "type-writer" (the person who operates a "typewriting machine").

At first Cora was only a type-writer. The Macdonald office operated in a curiously laborious way. Letters would be dictated to a male shorthand writer who took them down in his notebook. He then transcribed his notes into longhand and passed the draft to Cora, who typed the final version.

The firm's offices were on the second floor of the Merchants' Bank on the corner of Main and Lombard Streets, and Cora's desk was in the front room where she could see the visitors who came in. From the first she took a lively interest in the concerns of the firm. Much of the business was connected with the buying and selling of land, and Cora soon came to know the businessmen who were the clients. She greeted them by name, remembered the details of their transactions and often recalled the contents of important papers so accurately that there was no need to refer to them. Although she had been taken on simply as a typist, very soon she was performing as a highly competent secretary.

She stayed with Macdonald and Tupper until 1893, except for a year and a half when she worked for another firm. They were happy, busy years—the foundation of a promising future for both Cora and the young lawyers. Macdonald would in later years be Sir Hugh John Macdonald, premier of Manitoba.

Tupper would become the Hon. W.J. Tupper, lieutenant-governor of the province. But in the 1880s they were just young lawyers starting up in business and glad to have the efficient Cora Hind working for them.

Cora's work was not confined to office hours. She and her Aunt Alice both became active members of the Women's Christian Temperance Union when Letitia Youmans, its founder, visited Winnipeg in 1883 and set up a branch there. In fact, even before Mrs. Youmans's visit, there had been a move afoot to control the sale of liquor in the city. And with good reason.

As soon as the westward migration had begun, liquor traders had realized that a

Hugh John Macdonald, premier of Manitoba in 1900

profitable new market was opening up, and they had been quick to take advantage of it. At the height of the boom, although Winnipeg was still quite a small town, it had eighty-six hotels, plus sixty-four grocery stores that sold whisky. None of these establishments ever lacked customers, for construction workers had nothing much to do in the evenings except drink. There were no cinemas, and of course no radio or television. In any case, a good many of the men were single and had no homes to go to. They lived in tents or slept in rows on the saloon floors. Some of them slept in the streets where they had fallen down drunk and passed out. This happened so frequently that in winter a wagon-driver was hired to pick up the unconscious bodies and trundle them off to jail so that they would not freeze to death in the night.

Drunkenness was such a serious problem in early Winnipeg that it touched every branch of society. It affected

This anti-liquor cartoon was featured on the cover of the March 17, 1888 issue of Grip *magazine*

business—far too many men did not show up for work. It affected public safety—there was a high crime rate and frequent brawls. It even made shopping unpleasant, at times hazardous. The grocery stores were more like taverns than shops. Not only could you buy whisky, but you could perch on a bale or sack and drink it right there. Children sent to the local store to get five cents worth of sugar were often caught up in fights. Women shoppers were subjected to lewd remarks and sometimes accosted. Husbands who went to buy a sack of carrots might return home hours later, without the carrots, without their wages and with a dangerous amount of liquor inside them.

In these circumstances, it was only natural that the WCTU, which had started out simply as a temperance movement, would quickly turn its attention to the results of intemperance. A horrifying number of men, when drunk, beat up their wives and children. There was no law against it. A man could do pretty well what he wanted to his family, provided he did not actually kill them. He could also spend all his earnings—and his wife's—on drink. According to the law, everything a woman owned or earned belonged to her husband.

In marriages where the wife was the stronger character or where there was a bond of love or a sense of duty, women did not suffer noticeably from this law. Cora and her Aunt Alice had certainly not been mistreated by their male relatives. In fact, Cora had done better than her brothers, for she was her grandfather's favourite. But that was all the more reason why she felt the need to work for those who had not been so fortunate. It seemed to her appallingly unfair that men should have so many rights and women so few. Other members of the WCTU felt this too, and before long the union was championing the female cause on all fronts and calling for the right of women to vote so that they could have a say in the running of the country.

They were not the first Winnipeggers to take up this cause. There was a large Icelandic community in the area, and the Icelandic women had formed their own suffrage club. In Iceland they had been allowed to vote, but when they immigrated to Canada they found that women did not have this right. Cora and her friends agreed with the aims of the Icelandic women, and they became allies in the fight for female suffrage as well as for temperance.

The leader of both causes in Winnipeg was Dr. Amelia Yeomans (a near namesake of Letitia Youmans, the founder of the WCTU). The second-in-command of both causes was Cora Hind. Dr. Yeomans was president of the Winnipeg branch of the WCTU; Cora was treasurer and "superintendent for franchise." When they formed the Manitoba Equal Suffrage Club, Dr. Yeomans was elected president, and Cora Hind was elected vice-president. They worked closely together until Dr. Yeomans moved to Calgary in 1905.

The founding executive of the Manitoba Equal Suffrage Club, c. 1900. E. Cora Hind is seated at left, Dr. Amelia Yeomans, at right. The portrait is of Lucy Stone.

Dr. Yeomans was a remarkable woman and she had a strong influence on young Cora. She was living proof of what could be achieved. After her husband's death, she had enrolled in school at Ann Arbor, Michigan, to study medicine. She was over forty when she became a doctor. Then, in the 1880s, she and one of her daughters (who had also studied at Ann Arbor) set up a practice in Winnipeg—the first women physicians in the city.

Although Amelia Yeomans was a woman doctor and was expected to treat only women

and children, she quickly built up a reputation among all sections of the community. The motto of her suffrage association was "Peace on earth, good will towards men," and she put this motto into practice. Politicians, clergymen and businessmen often found themselves working with her to improve conditions in the city. Some even agreed to support female suffrage—or at least not to speak against it. The police also cooperated with Dr. Yeomans. The poor looked to her for aid, and even criminals turned to her. On one occasion a condemned man asked to see her, rather than a priest, before his execution.

Amelia Yeomans had an especially large following among the needy, for she made it her business to look into areas that most well-to-do citizens did not bother about. She inspected the prisons and pronounced them to be shockingly unhealthy—badly ventilated, over-crowded and infested with lice and cockroaches. She spoke out against conditions in clothing factories where women slaved long hours for desperately low wages in stuffy, ill-lit rooms. She campaigned fiercely against prostitution, warning both men and women about the dangers of venereal disease. She spoke out on this subject in such detail that for a time she lost the support of the clergy. Nevertheless, she carried on as forcefully as ever, whether it

A Winnipeg slum in the early 1900s

First Typist in the West

was to urge a greater tolerance towards non-English immigrants, to call for a change in the liquor laws or to demand better housing for the poor. There was hardly an aspect of city life that did not feel her impact. When she died in 1913, Cora Hind wrote: "There should be a life-sized portrait of Dr. Amelia Yeomans placed in the city hall, for it is very questionable if any worshipful mayor whose portrait now adorns the walls ever did one tithe as much for the real upbuilding of the city."

One of the pledge cards of the Women's Christian Temperance Union

Cora herself was far more than an observer in all these activities. She accompanied Dr. Yeomans through the factories and prisons. As often as not, she then wrote a report on their findings and submitted it to the *Free Press*. Not all her pieces were published, but many were.

Whenever Dr. Yeomans made a speech, Cora made sure that the *Free Press* received an account of that too; and she sometimes wrote speeches for fellow WCTU members who knew what they wanted to say but could not phrase it easily.

It is likely that Cora was overworking during these years—busy all day in the office, busy at weekends and in the evenings. She fell an easy victim to typhoid, "Red River Fever" as it was called. Typhoid epidemics were common, for the city's water was far from pure. Only about 500 houses in Winnipeg were provided with main drainage. Most houses had privies, and unserviceable ones at that. Consequently, ditches degenerated into open drains and the river easily became contaminated. Since drinking water was taken from the river and delivered to the houses in wagons, disease spread rapidly. It was only after 1904, when there was a particularly severe typhoid epidemic, that the city council installed an efficient sewage system. But that was too late to save Cora from catching typhoid.

She was delirious for days. She became so weak that her Aunt Alice feared she was going to die. At last the crisis passed, and slowly Cora began to recover, though she did not fully regain her strength. The following year she fell sick with pneumonia. Clearly, she was run down and still very weak. All that winter, Aunt Alice greeted her anxiously with a glass of steaming milk on her return from the office.

Late nineteenth century handbill distributed by the WCTU

The office staff were as concerned about Cora as Aunt Alice. They were fond of their clerk-typewriter and they respected her. All along, they had been following her activities with interest, though there had been some teasing at first, especially about Cora's temperance work. Clerks who enjoyed drinking considered the whole business rather a joke. But even the most patronizing became proud of Cora Hind once her pieces began to appear in the newspaper. On a slack day, they might find her, head down, brow furrowed, as she composed a speech or drew up an agenda for the next WCTU meeting. It was impossible to work in that office and not be aware of the arguments in favour of temperance.

Of course, Hugh John Macdonald was already aware of the harmful effects of alcohol. His father was not the most sober of characters. But it may have been the influence of Cora's work as much as his home background that led him to introduce a bill prohibiting the sale of liquor when he became premier of Manitoba in 1900. The Macdonald Act, as it was later called, seemed a triumph for the prohibitionists, but shortly after it received royal assent, Macdonald resigned his premiership in order to run for a federal seat. Rodmond Roblin, who succeeded him, drew many of his votes from liquor suppliers and tavern owners, and he managed to get the act disallowed. So prohibition did not come into force. Even so, Cora and her fellow workers now had good reason to believe that conditions would eventually improve and that Winnipeg would not be known forever as "the vice capital of the West." Already the city was a more civilized place than it had been when Cora first arrived. There were amateur concerts and theatricals, clubs for working men and improved conditions for working women.

There was a notable improvement for one working woman in particular. Long before Hugh John Macdonald became premier, his clerk-typewriter decided to go it alone. In 1893 Cora Hind went to see her bank manager, borrowed a modest sum of money that would take her years to repay, rented an office and set up her own stenographer's bureau. Needless to say, it was the first public stenographer's bureau in the West. It was also the means by which E. Cora Hind would make her way into journalism.

Chapter 4

The Way into Journalism

S ince Cora Hind was the only public stenographer in Winnipeg, many people called on her services. There were visiting prospectors and businessmen, farmers and merchants, even a circus manager. Most of them were keen to chat about their work, and Cora was always glad to listen. She was intensely curious about everything that was going on, for these were exciting times. During the 1880s and especially during the 1890s, the whole of western Canada was being transformed.

The Northwest Rebellion had made one thing very clear to the country's politicians: an underpopulated West was an unreliable West. More settlers were needed, and quickly. After the CPR was completed, increasing western grain trade, wheat merchants, stockbrokers and bankers established offices there. Manufacturers moved in to make and sell agricultural imple-

This drawing shows a prairie farm after three years of settlement

ments. Wholesale and retail businesses were set up to serve the farmers. The entire city acquired a new lease on life. To be sure, Winnipeg was still a boisterous frontier town, but it was no longer only the gateway to the West. Winnipeg was the West, the focal point for a vast hinterland.

Cora was fascinated by all this activity, for she could actually see it happening. Each week the trains trundled past, packed with immigrants. Each week she could read in the paper about the new land that was being opened. And each week she was visited in her office by people who were actively involved in the developments—the brokers, cattlemen and wheat farmers who came to have their typing done.

Having been brought up on a farm, Cora was particularly interested in what the farmers had to tell her, and it became their custom to discuss their affairs with her. "From every one of them I learned something," she said. They also learned from her. She had a particularly good memory and could rattle off figures and statistics without looking them up. As time passed, Cora Hind's office

Clifford Sifton

Clifford Sifton's immigration program attracted a flood of new settlers in the late 1890s

These grains and grasses were grown in
MANITOBA • CANADA
Cheap but productive lands can be acquired in Manitoba on very reasonable terms
For further information, pamphlets and maps apply to
IMMIGRATION & COLONIZATION BRANCH
Province of Manitoba
439 MAIN ST. WINNIPEG

Settlers arriving at the Winnipeg train station in 1897

became known as a place where you could get the latest information on everything from cattle to mining rights. On one occasion she gave a visiting British diplomat such a comprehensive description of western Canada that he paid her twice over—once for the typing and once for the lecture on Canadian affairs.

It was therefore, hardly surprising that members of the Manitoba Dairy Association approached Cora Hind when they needed a secretary for a convention they were holding. She had done work for many of the dairymen, and they knew how competent she was. They probably also knew that she would write an account of their meeting for the newspaper. It was no secret that she had set her heart on becoming a reporter. Her application for a staff position was permanently on file at the *Manitoba Free Press*.

Cora took full advantage of the opportunity and did send a report of the convention to the *Free Press*. This was the first of

many meetings that she was to attend—and report on.
Meanwhile, the dairymen's association had realized that it needed
someone to handle routine affairs on a day-to-day basis, someone
who would keep track of price changes and notify the creameries
and cheese factories. Cora willingly agreed to do this, and she
was appointed secretary of the association.

In spite of these new duties, Cora continued to run her
stenographer's bureau. Her position with the dairymen was in
effect a part-time job, but it was of special significance for it
gave her the opportunity to write more frequently for the *Free
Press*. Her reports on marketing began to appear regularly, as
did her accounts of stock shows, agricultural fairs and other
events that she attended as the farmers' representative.
Although very much a freelance journalist, she was making a
name for herself.

Her growing fame can be judged by her visit to Manitou
early in the 1890s. Her arrival was announced in advance by
the local paper, and there was a large crowd at the station when
she arrived. In the crowd was a teenaged schoolmistress who
hoped to be a writer one day and who was eager to get a
glimpse of Winnipeg's lady reporter. "I knew about Miss
Hind," she explained. "She wrote signed articles, interviews,
spoke in public." The young schoolmistress was beside herself
with excitement when at last Cora Hind stepped down from
the train:

*There she was. No mistake, a young woman in a tan tweed
suit with brown facings; a little hat to match with a saucy quill set
at exactly the right angle; and a scarf with flaring ends … Her
face had a fresh and lovely color and her fine dark blue eyes beamed
with health and friendliness—a break in the crowd gave me a full
view of her as she stepped briskly down the steps, with her small
square leather bag in her hand. Then it was I saw her little feet so
trimly shod in russet leather shoes. I had never seen prettier shoes.
The crowd drew back making an aisle for her, closing in behind as
she passed …*

*I had seen her! I had seen what a newspaper woman could be
at her shining best.*

The young teacher who wrote this was called Nellie
Mooney. Later, as Nellie McClung, author and suffragette, she

too would draw crowds of admirers when she visited small country towns. But at the time she was too shy even to speak to the famous Cora Hind.

Cora Hind's reputation was not confined to the West or even to Canada. American journals also took her stories. She became so sure of herself that when one American magazine tried to publish an article under the name "E.C. Hind," she refused to allow it. "E. Cora Hind" it must be—to show that the writer was a woman. Otherwise the article must be returned to her. She had come a long way since the days when she was willing to have her work published anonymously.

Cora was writing on a great range of subjects at this time, even doing book reviews, though for the most part she concentrated on marketing and agriculture, the subjects she was most interested in. Many of her pieces were printed in the trade journals that Colonel John Bayne Maclean published from his offices in Montreal and Toronto. Maclean had not yet launched the magazine that was to be known by his name, but he was already a prominent figure in the publishing world. He ran a number of journals, such as *Canadian Grocer, Dry Goods Review, Printer and Publisher* and *Bookseller and Stationer.* "As a commercial editor," said one admirer, "he has perhaps no superior in the Canadian press." It was therefore a great compliment to Cora when in 1895 Maclean invited her to become his western correspondent.

Cora accepted enthusiastically. Here at last was formal recognition of her work as a journalist. Even so, she could not afford to close her stenographer's office. As she pointed out, "Trade journals are fair pay and sure, but not always prompt." Nevertheless, it was due to her work for Maclean's Publications that she had her first big chance. This took place in 1898, a year that was to be a turning point in her life.

It had been a depressing autumn on the prairies. There had been rain and more rain, so much rain that threshing could not begin until October 6. That was far too late in the season, and stories of gloom and doom were spreading out of the West: the crop would be a disaster; most of the wheat would be frozen before it could be harvested. The situation looked so hopeless that eastern businessmen stopped shipping goods west. They did not think westerners would be able to pay for them.

In the midst of this pessimism, Colonel Maclean decided to

discover what the true picture was. Were the rumours exaggerated or would the crop really be a failure? He sent a wire to his western correspondent and asked her to find out.

Cora Hind left Winnipeg the evening she received Maclean's telegram. She bought a ticket to Moose Jaw and set off by train, breaking her journey at the stops along the way. At each station where she alighted, her procedure was the same. First she went to the town's livery barn to hire a rig and driver (the equivalent of a limousine service). Then she drove out through the wide prairie farmlands, a small, determined figure dwarfed by the huge skies. North of the railway she drove, south of the railway, east and west, covering as much of each area as she could.

She had not yet taken to wearing the well-known jacket and riding breeches, so it was in a long and cumbersome tweed skirt and neat, buttoned boots that she waded through the mud and into the fields. Sometimes one glance was enough. The blackened, rain-sodden stooks told her all she needed to know.

A parade of binders was a common feature of the harvesting season in the 1890s

The Way into Journalism

Other fields looked more promising, but Cora Hind was not content merely to look. She gathered up handfuls of wheat and threshed the heads in her hand. Then she counted the kernels. Sometimes when she pressed them between her fingers, out spurted water—frozen wheat. But on many farms she found nice plump heads of grain. Despite the rain the overall picture was not as desperate as the rumours had suggested. When Cora Hind returned to Winnipeg, she was able to wire Colonel Maclean that although about 35,000 acres were frozen, an average crop could be expected.

Maclean immediately published this report. Confidence was restored, for Maclean had a reputation for getting at the facts. His market reports were considered so reliable that they were used in compiling government statistics and were even accepted as evidence in court cases. So, when he published his western correspondent's findings, tension relaxed and business-men started shipping their goods west again. They did not regret it. When all the wheat had been harvested, it proved to be an average yield—just as Cora Hind had predicted.

Cora Hind's credit rose considerably as a result of her crop forecast. A woman writer she might be, but obviously she knew her subject. Editors across the country became eager to print her work, and she was only too willing to provide them with material. Reporting began to claim more and more of her time. Often Aunt Alice would hold the fort at the stenographer's bureau while her niece covered a cattle auction or some other function. Although Alice Hind could not type, she could greet the clients and take in work. And sometimes she made surveys of her own. She was especially interested in real estate and used to inspect houses for sale and provide Cora with material for articles on the subject.

Cora became so busy that she had a hard time fitting in her typing work. She was writing almost as much as a full-time journalist, not only contributing to Maclean's Publications and other magazines, but also producing a regular column on mar-keting for the *Free Press*. It was a continual grievance to her that the *Free Press* had not taken her on staff. She had been deeply hurt some years earlier when a journalist named Agnes Laut had been given a job on the paper, while she, an earlier applicant, had been left out in the cold. But she was not to be left out for much longer.

In 1901 there was a change of leadership at the *Free Press*, and John Wesley Dafoe was brought in from Montreal as editor. Although Dafoe had been on the staff of the *Free Press* between 1886 and 1892, he had not recognized Cora's talent. At that time she had still been a clerk-typist for Macdonald and Tupper. Though she had had articles published occasionally, most of her pieces had been about temperance issues. They were not considered of great importance.

When Dafoe returned to Winnipeg, he found a very different situation. As he later said to Cora Hind:

> *When after some years I came back to the* Free Press *in 1901, I found that, as part of your activities in a business which you were then conducting, you were supplying the* Free Press *regularly with reports dealing with agricultural and marketing matters. The wisdom of having you an all-time member of the staff was so evident that an arrangement to this end was soon made.*

One of Dafoe's first acts as editor was to call Cora Hind to his office and offer her a job.

So it was that almost twenty years after she had first applied, E. Cora Hind was appointed to the staff of the *Manitoba Free Press*. At long last she had arrived. But this was not in any sense the end of the road. It was just the beginning.

Chapter 5
Editor and Crop Forecaster

E. Cora Hind's title was Commercial Editor to the *Manitoba Free Press*. Later this was changed to Commercial and Agricultural Editor, but in fact her duties did not change. From the first, it was taken for granted that she would handle all matters connected with farming. And that is exactly what she proceeded to do.

Eagerly she settled into her office and began to organize her department. Few people can ever have tackled a job with such enthusiasm. While continuing her work for the Dairy Association and her column on marketing, she branched out into areas that had not previously been covered by the paper—for instance, gathering statistics on beef production. Cora Hind had found it shocking that during the Northwest Rebellion beef had been brought in from the East to feed the troops. That sort of thing would not happen again. Cattle were shipped out of the West these days. Thanks to the arrival of so many settlers, the prairies had become the great farmland of the Dominion.

Beef cattle, dairy cows, hogs and even sheep were being raised by the thousands. But wheat was still the chief product, and it demanded the main attention of the commercial editor. Most of the new settlers sowed their cultivated land with wheat, and by the time Cora Hind joined the *Free Press*, more than 1.6 million hectares had been planted. Ten years later, in 1911, there were more than four and a half million hectares of wheat fields in the prairies. The number of hectares doubled again in the next ten years.

This great increase was not only because so many settlers were breaking new land but also because individual farms were larger than they had been in earlier years. During the latter part of the nineteenth century, agriculture had become mecha-

nized as more and more machines had been invented to do work that formerly had been done by hand. By 1901 there had been a revolution in farming methods, though the major advance (the use of gasoline-powered vehicles) did not take place until World War I. Until then, some of the machinery was powered by steam engines, using straw as fuel. But more often, horsepower was literally horse power. Even the combine harvester-thresher, "the most wonderful of modern harvest machinery," was drawn by teams of horses.

The combine required considerable horse power until gasoline engines revolutionized farm machinery

During Cora Hind's first years at the *Free Press*, this early form of combine was more common in the United States than in Canada. Most Canadian farmers used self-binding harvesters and then threshed the grain with steam-powered threshers. But even the self-binder was considered pretty remarkable. In 1911 W.P. Rutter wrote an admiring description in his book, *Wheat Growing in Canada, the United States and Argentina:*

> The self-binding harvester is a machine which delivers the grain bound in sheaves. It can easily be adjusted to variations in the grain and to the surface of the wheat field ... One man and three horses can harvest with the binder from 10 to 20 acres [4 to 8 hectares] per day, and two men are necessary to set up the sheaves. In North-West Canada the harvesting is done by self-binders, of which there are three sizes, cutting respectively 6, 7, and 8 feet [1.8, 2 and 2.4 metre] swaths.

½ MILE FURROW STRAIGHT AS AN ARROW

Mechanized farm machinery was powered by steam engines before the First World War

Such machines, though primitive by today's standards, allowed farmers to cultivate larger areas of land. And since more and more farmers were working the prairies, wheat production soared—from 55 million bushels when Cora Hind joined the *Free Press* to 230 million only ten years later. By the end of World War I, so much wheat was being grown that it had become Canada's major export.

At the same time, improved varieties of wheat were being developed. For many years Red Fife had been the most popular grain, but it had drawbacks. Although it did well in the prairie soil and had good milling qualities, it did not mature quickly enough for the growing season in the West. Too often the crop was damaged by frost before it could be harvested.

Even before her appointment to the *Free Press*, Cora Hind had been following the research of Dr. William Saunders, the director of the Dominion's experimental farms. He had been cross-fertilizing various strains of wheat in an effort to find a variety that was suited to the prairie climate. In 1903 his son Charles Edward Saunders was appointed Dominion Cerealist so that he could continue his father's experiments. By 1906 he had developed a type of wheat that matured between a week and ten days earlier than Red Rife. It gave a good yield, produced a high-quality bread and seemed to be an all-round winner. Saunders called it Marquis Wheat.

In 1907 approximately twelve kilograms of Marquis were sent to the experimental farm at Indian Head, and there Cora Hind was able to inspect the new strain herself and report on how well it was doing. Another batch, sent to the Brandon experimental farm the following year, did equally well. Before long, millions of acres across the prairies were being sown with Marquis. The new grain proved an overwhelming success, and wheat production increased dramatically.

Marquis's only weakness was that it was not resistant to the disease known as rust. (Even today the disease is still a threat, in spite of the development of certain "rust-resistant" varieties.) Rust is a fungus that attacks many species of grasses, including the grains. Since the organism that causes it cannot survive a cold winter, it had been no great threat to Canadian farmers when wheat had been grown only in the eastern provinces. Nor was it at first a problem in the West. But the unsheltered prairie fields were more vulnerable than farms in Ontario and Quebec, for the rust spores could be carried on the winds that blew unobstructed up the central plains from the warm lands of the American South. This is what happened in the summer of 1904, the first year the prairies experienced an epidemic of rust.

That summer was exceptionally hot and humid, ideal conditions for the blight. Appearing first in southern Manitoba, it spread quickly. Farm after farm was infected. A group of

Harvesting Red Fife grain in 1903

American experts who visited Canada that year declared that the crop would be a failure. The most one could hope for would be 35 million bushels, they said.

Cora Hind was in her office at the *Free Press* when she read their report in a Chicago newspaper. Only 35 million bushels! It was impossible. Even allowing for the damage done by rust, it was impossible. She marched straight into Editor Dafoe's office, brandishing the newspaper indignantly.

"What exactly does this mean?" asked Dafoe cautiously.

"It means," said Cora Hind, "that the business of 'killing the crop' is in full swing. It means that for speculative purposes, Chicago has decided that the Canadian crop is ruined."

In many ways it was a repeat of the situation in 1898. Once again there was loss of confidence in the western crop, and once again the same solution presented itself. Cora Hind must make a survey and report on the true situation.

But things were a little different this time. Wheat had become such an important export that the nation as a whole stood to lose if brokers believed the western crop was going to fail. And as Cora Hind realized, rival grain dealers south of the border stood to gain. There was another problem too. The Chicago papers had quoted a figure: 35 million bushels. It would not be enough for a Winnipeg newspaper to predict "an average yield." It too would have to come up with a figure.

Cora Hind agreed to provide a definite figure, and she set off on her survey with crusading zeal. As before, she took the train and then hired a horse and buggy at each stop—sometimes teams of horses. She set herself an exhausting schedule, driving from dawn to dusk along the rough tracks that served as roads. Time and again the wheels of her rig would get stuck in a rut, and then she or the driver would have to walk to the nearest farm for help. But she carried on determinedly right across the prairies until she had inspected enough farms to be able to estimate the crop with some accuracy. When she returned to Winnipeg, she boldly announced that the Chicago figure was way below the mark. The West could expect a yield of about 55 million bushels.

The *Free Press* immediately published this estimate. Other newspapers copied it, and to some extent confidence was restored. But the Americans remained skeptical. When a month later Cora Hind visited the Duluth Grain Exchange and was introduced as "the 55-million-bushel lady," she was greeted by more jeers than cheers. During the following months she waited anxiously for the harvesting to be completed. Then she had to wait again while the crop was totalled up. But then came her moment of glory. The official count was 54 million bushels, only one million less than she had predicted—and 19 million more than the Chicago figure.

In later years she said that this first estimate for the *Free Press* was beginner's luck, but in fact nearly all her forecasts were extraordinarily accurate. From then on, she surveyed the crop every summer, and she continued to do so until she was seventy-two years old. The only years she missed were 1912, when there was so much rain that even an approximate estimate was impossible, and 1926, when she had to break off halfway through because of an attack of appendicitis.

Her predictions so regularly proved correct that grain handlers across the world came to rely on them. No dealer would make a move until he had read E. Cora Hind's annual crop estimate. This was printed in the *Free Press* each September and was kept a closely guarded secret until it was published. Speculators might try to get just a hint of what it was likely to be, but Cora Hind would not breathe a word, not for love nor money. If she had been unprincipled, she could have made a fortune by leaking advance information. But she was a scrupulously honest person, and in any case, she had no wish to betray the West.

Nor would she change her report to suit anyone. Her forecast in 1913 was considered disastrously low, bad for business and bad for Canada—as indeed it was. When her estimate was printed, there was an outcry against "Calamity Cora." As editor of the paper, Dafoe also came under attack and pressure was put on him to change the report. It is not known who approached him, but it was said to be "a very important person indeed." However, Dafoe refused to alter the figures. He stuck by his agricultural expert, and she stuck by her forecast. Her survey across the prairies had indicated a very poor crop, and in all honesty she could not predict a good one. "No one loves the West more passionately than I do," she said. "But very early in my newspaper career I learned that the West was big enough and strong enough to have the truth told about it on all occasions." Both Cora Hind and Dafoe were justified when

John Wesley Dafoe

harvesting was completed. The yield was almost exactly what she had predicted.

Many people found it amazing that anyone, let alone a woman, should be able to make such reliable estimates. The *London Morning Post* expressed the general feeling of surprise and admiration:

> *It would be strange enough to us if a man of great experience could soberly and accurately forecast the crop—not just make a flukey guess, not just once be lucky, but time after time get nearer to the inner future truth than anyone else. But that this faculty would be centered in a woman—this for some reason seems extraordinary.*

How did Cora Hind do it? The skeptics said that she used to march into a field, spin around three times with her eyes shut, then grab a head of wheat and make her pronouncement. The truth was rather less dramatic. She did take wheat samples from various parts of a field—but with her eyes open. And it was with her eyes open that she counted the kernels and checked their fullness. Then, having judged the quality of the grain, she would gaze across the field and know, simply by looking, approximately how much it would yield. It was not guesswork as much as informed conjecture based on a thorough knowledge of wheat and a thorough knowledge of farming. And of course it was also based on experience. Each year she was covering much the same territory, so she was able to compare the fields with their appearance on previous surveys. Moreover, she followed the progress of the wheat throughout the year. Farmers kept in touch with her. Correspondents in the three prairie provinces checked on the crop and reported to her. She was given a great deal of help. But it was she alone who inspected the farms during the key months of July and August. And though others helped her add up the figures and cross-check the calculations, it was she alone who was responsible for the final estimate.

She took little credit for her work. When asked about the surveys, she was more likely to praise her many assistants, especially the drivers who took her over the bumpy roads on her inspection tours. And she always gave special credit to the Free Press for financing the surveys, a very costly business.

"Far too much has been made of the personal factor in the annual crop estimate," she once said. "It is true that I first suggested it and that I have been personally associated with it ever since. But hardly ever is it pointed out that this is a splendid example of public service on the part of the paper ... The *Free Press* serves its community in many ways, but this is a special service we have chosen to make to the West. I always say that there are three things the public never begins to pay the value of. They are bread, milk, and the daily paper."

Examples of the Wheat Survey

YEAR	CORA HIND'S ESTIMATE	ACTUAL CROP
1904	55 000 000 bushels	54 000 000 bushels
1905	85 000 000 bushels	84 506 857 bushels
1907	71 250 000 bushels	70 922 584 bushels
1909	118 109 000 bushels	118 119 000 bushels

Typically, she did not add that she was a major contributor in all three areas, and in other branches of agriculture too. She made it her business to know of anything and everything that was happening that might even remotely be connected with farming. Her office was one of the busiest at the *Free Press*. There was hardly a farmers' meeting or cattle sale anywhere in western Canada that she did not attend. She even gave her support to local ploughing matches; and several times each year she visited the Department of Agriculture in Ottawa, packing an enormously full schedule into a few days.

"Her routine never varied," wrote the *Free Press* correspondent in Ottawa. "In the course of three days she would see perhaps 60 people, beginning each day at 7 a.m., and knocking off after midnight. She was never content to talk only with the higher ups. She always sought out the men who were doing the actual work—scientists in their greenhouses, pathologists in their labs. Strangely, whenever a new idea was being born— crested wheat grass, breeding regulations, and so on—Miss Hind turned up to give a hand. And she usually stood guard until the baby was firmly established."

As a newspaperwoman, E. Cora Hind's main role was to report on what was happening and to publicize any new developments in agriculture. But she did far more than this. She considered it her duty to promote Canadian agriculture in every way possible. For instance, when she attended meetings of the Western Canada Livestock Union, it was as a participant as much as a reporter. She took part in the discussions, gave lectures on improved methods of raising hogs or cattle and served on special committees. Similarly, she was a founding member of the Canadian Co-operative Wool Growers—she helped to draft its bylaws, became one of its shareholders and served several terms as a director.

The dairy industry continued to receive her support and her active participation. One of her most triumphant moments was when a Saskatchewan cow won a world record. The cow was named Canary Korndyke Alcartra, and during a 305-day test it had produced more milk containing a higher percentage of butterfat than any cow had done before. Cora Hind wrote an enthusiastic article praising Canary Korndyke Alcartra. Then she sat back, shot a whimsical glance at her colleagues and produced a typical E. Cora Hind remark. "The labour of years has not been entirely thrown away," she announced. "Several members of the *Free Press* editorial department are now vaguely aware that milk does not originate in bottles."

The staff were used to their agricultural editor's pithy comments and, indeed, enjoyed them. Whether Cora Hind was speaking or writing, she had a way of going to the heart of the matter in a few straight sentences. Usually she did so without malice, but she could be witheringly sarcastic on occasion. Those who roused her enmity did so at their own risk.

Cora Hind's ability with words was to prove a valuable asset when, after more than a decade at the *Free Press*, she once again turned her attention to the subject of women's rights—just before the movement gained new strength. This time the campaign was waged by an association known as the Political Equality League. Needless to say, E. Cora Hind was one of its founding members.

Chapter 6
Working for Women – and Men

E. Cora Hind was a great "club" person. She enjoyed belonging to societies, speaking at meetings, making resolutions—and carrying them out. It was her way of getting things done. In addition to the many farming associations she belonged to (generally as the only woman), she was one of the founding members of the Canadian Women's Press Club. And in 1908 she and some friends formed the Quill Club, an informal literary group of both men and women, who met in each other's homes in order "to talk shop, to get into print and to be paid for being there."

The second general meeting of the Canadian Women's Press Club in June 1906. Cora Hind is in a white dress at the centre of the second row.

41

Shortly after the Quill Club was formed, the members were given a talk by Nellie McClung, who was no longer an unknown schoolteacher. Her first novel, *Sowing Seeds in Danny*, was fast becoming a bestseller. Since that day back in the 1890s when Nellie had caught her first glimpse of Winnipeg's famous newspaperwoman, she too had been making a name for herself, and she had met Cora Hind and formed a close friendship with her. Cora Hind generally stayed with the McClungs when she visited Manitou. She was treated as one of the family. Nellie McClung was given an equally warm welcome when she came to Winnipeg. In spite of an age difference of more than ten years, it was natural that the two would become friends. Not only were they both writers, but both were strong supporters of women's rights and prohibition.

Cora Hind had not given up either cause since her first surge of activity in the 1880s. Although her journalism had taken top priority, she had continued to press for prohibition and to lobby various provincial ministers on the issue of female suffrage. Her approach to them had been characteristically formal, neatly typed and very much to the point:

> *I would like, if possible, to obtain a serious and candid reply to the following questions:*
>
> *1. Do you believe in the right of franchise for women?*
> *2. If not, why not?*
> *3. If you believe in the right of women to the franchise or suffrage, are you willing that they should receive it on precisely the same terms as it is now granted to men?*
> *4. If in opposition to the suffrage being extended to women, what amount of study have you given to the question and on what do you specially base your objection?*
> *5. What weight do you attach to petitions in matters of this kind?*
>
> *I trust you will not consider the asking of these questions a liberty and that you will have the kindness and patience to answer them.*

She did receive answers to her circulars, though they were not always as candid as she would have liked. While Premier and Agriculture Minister Thomas Greenway assured her that he personally was in favour of granting the franchise to women, he concluded his letter by remarking: "I must say that it has not been made very clear to me that there is any very general demand upon the part of the women of the Province for this privilege."

Cora Hind answered the cautious politician with her usual directness:

> **Dear Sir:**
> *I am in receipt of yours of the 4th inst. Allow me to thank you for your prompt and courteous reply.*
> *I note what you say re not having been shown that the women of the Province are really anxious for the reform. It will be the duty of myself and fellow-workers to endeavor to bring before your Legislature, at its next sitting, convincing proof that we are in earnest in this matter.*
> *But in order that we may do this most efficiently, would it be troubling you too much to enquire, what is the best method, failing petitions, to bring this matter before the Legislature? I make this inquiry because all the members, from whom I have heard up to date, agree in stating that petitions are of little weight.*
> *I have the honor to be*
> *Sir,*
> *Your obedient servant,*
> *E. Cora Hind*
> *Local Supt. of Franchise.*

As a result of these efforts, the Manitoba government introduced a franchise bill in 1894. But it never received a second reading. And in succeeding years, although the suffrage issue remained alive, it certainly did not flourish. Not until the McClung family came to live in Winnipeg in 1911, that is.

Nellie McClung arrived in a crusading mood and proceeded to make per presence felt. She was a far more fiery character than Cora Hind—no more determined, but more impetuous. Cora Hind's approach tended to be formal and polite, though she never hesitated to say what she thought. Over the years she had gained in confidence. She was no longer an eager young woman trying to make her way in the world. In her forties she was the Cora Hind that her associates remember—kindly and very considerate to her many friends but a rather awesome figure who did not suffer fools gladly. However, even at her most outspoken, she tried to be well mannered. By contrast, Nellie McClung was prepared to be brash to the point of rudeness if she felt that a cause demanded it. She did not in the least mind giving sharp answers to evasive politicians.

Nellie began her campaign in Winnipeg fairly quietly. In 1912 she and Cora Hind and several other women (including Kennethe Haig and Lillian Beynon Thomas, both editorial writers for the *Free Press*) formed the Political Equality League with the specific purpose of getting women the vote. They were supported by the WCTU, the Women's Labour League, the Icelandic Women's Suffrage Association and, significantly, the Grain Growers' Association.

During 1913 they kept the suffrage issue in the public eye, and their movement gained in popularity. But the premier, Sir Rodmond Roblin, would have no part in female franchise. He considered it a serious mistake that would break up homes and "throw children into the arms of servant girls." Most women were too emotional, he maintained. Their temperament was not suited to politics. Even when Nellie McClung called on him personally, he refused to take her seriously, remarking: "Why do women want to mix in the hurly-burly of politics? My mother was the best woman in the world, and she certainly never wanted to vote."

Tobias Crawford Norris

Clearly, Nellie McClung and her associates could expect no help from the government. So they turned to the opposition and approached the Liberal leader, T.C. Norris. Norris was willing to listen, partly perhaps because he realized that the Political Equality League had a large following. He agreed to include female suffrage in his campaign program during the forthcoming election.

Working for Women – and Men

Meanwhile, the suffragettes were rallying their forces. A few months before the election, in January 1914, they staged a Mock Parliament at the Walker Theatre in Winnipeg, pretending that women were the favoured sex and that it was men who were seeking the right to vote. Nellie McClung acted the role of premier, blatantly mimicking Roblin and parodying his more emotional statements. The irony was not lost on the audience, and the comedy played several nights to packed houses. The *Winnipeg Telegram* as well as the *Free Press* reviewed the performance enthusiastically. Moreover, many in the audience found themselves being drawn into the cause. Suffrage pamphlets and a petition were passed around during the intermissions.

Nellie McClung worked passionately to establish the rights of women in Canada

Nellie McClung followed up this success by throwing herself wholeheartedly into the election campaign, touring the province and speaking from the hustings as a champion of the Liberals. In the election—which took place a year later—the Liberals won a landslide victory.

So now at long last Manitoba women would get the vote. But no, not quite yet. When T.C. Norris became premier, he discovered that he was not as keen on female suffrage as he had been during his days in the opposition. He was not sure that women really wanted the responsibility of voting. By this time the McClung family had moved to Edmonton, but Nellie McClung was in touch with her Manitoba friends. E. Cora Hind was still in Winnipeg, as were many other determined suffragettes, including Mary Crawford, a forceful Winnipeg doctor who was the new president of the Political Equality League. They set to work to raise petitions. Suffragettes and sympathizers across the province joined in the project. Premier Norris was left in no doubt that the women of the province wanted the franchise. He bowed to the inevitable, and in January 1916 Manitoba women finally gained the right to vote in provincial elections.

A few months later there was another victory. The Liberals' chief platform in the election campaign had been prohibition. Their rallying cry had been "Banish the bars!" Premier Norris was, therefore, committed to this cause too. In March he held a plebiscite on the issue, and when the voters came out heavily in favour of prohibition, he drew up the Manitoba Temperance Act. This act, which in effect banned the sale of liquor anywhere in the province, became law in June 1916.

And so it came about that after more than thirty years, the two causes that Cora Hind had been working for since her arrival in the West were finally victorious. Her part in both campaigns had been slow and steady—generally as second-in-command and organizer rather than leader. She was not the catalyst, the fiery element that actually brought about the change. That honour goes to Nellie McClung. Nevertheless, Cora Hind's own contribution may well have been more important in the long run because of the formidable reputation she had gained in what was still considered to be a masculine subject. Faced with E. Cora Hind, nobody could convincingly trot out the well-worn clichés about female emotionalism and frailty and frivolity. By her very existence, she was the strongest possible argument for the women's cause.

At each stage in her career, she had taken on "men's" jobs—and had done them better than men. Even as a young woman, she had moved straight into the male arena and had performed so competently that men had not questioned her right to be there. She was the first woman to be given a ticket to the floor of

The Manitoba Temperance Act of 1916 closed down liquor stores throughout the province

Working for Women – and Men

the Winnipeg Grain Exchange, the first woman to belong to the various farmers' associations, the first woman to take her place on the judge's stand at agricultural shows, and the only woman journalist in Canada to have her byline frequently over front-page news. E. Cora Hind daily promoted the cause of women, not merely by words but by performance.

The apartment at 34 Preston Court, where Cora Hind lived from 1911 to 1915

Yet for all this, she was a very moderate feminist by today's standards. She was even a moderate when compared to some of her contemporaries. It has been said that E. Cora Hind was a suffragette "in her own way," and this is possibly true. She believed passionately that women should have equal opportunities and that they should have equality before the law; and she was convinced that women were the superior gender. But it was not in her character to go to extremes to make her point. Logic was her tool, not extravagant gestures. She was certainly far too level-headed to indulge in the form of gender war that some suffragettes conducted. She knew that it was not men she disliked; it was their privileged position.

All her life Cora Hind got on extremely well with men. Most of her friends and associates were men, and she worked with them, not as a rival but as a colleague, concentrating on the job in hand. Yet she did not expect to be treated as a man socially. In many respects she approved of the conventions of her day.

Essentially, E. Cora Hind was a Victorian. Queen Victoria had been on the throne for the first forty years of her life, and Cora retained many Victorian values. For instance, she thought that women should be modest and chaste. On a personal level she took it for granted that men would assume the male role and that she would perform the female role, making the coffee or accepting conventional gallantries—a door opened for her, a chair pulled out. She believed in equality, but not in similarity. This was especially true in private life. Although she had chosen a career (and would defend any woman's right to do so), she saw woman's prime function to be that of homemaker. This does not mean that she thought women should be tied to the home. She often encouraged rural wives to get out and develop community programs, to play an active part in running their neighbourhoods. But at the same time she felt that they should not despise domestic work; a happy, well-run home was the foundation of a prosperous, healthy nation. Cooking, washing, sewing and creating a comfortable environment for husband and children—these were of paramount importance, and they were a woman's first duty. It would not have occurred to Cora Hind that men should share these tasks.

She herself loved to cook, and when she was out on the trail she made great friends with many of the farmers' wives, talking to them woman to woman, discussing bread-making, exchanging recipes or perhaps choosing dress materials. She took an almost exaggerated interest in her own clothing, which was one reason why she so enjoyed wearing her famous buckskin jacket. And of course she loved to knit. The click of her needles at conventions drove many a speaker to distraction.

E. Cora Hind, knitting in her apartment

Cora Hind's public knitting was not a pose. It was simply that she liked to use her time to the full. ("A woman's hands should never be idle" was a familiar Victorian saying.) In any case, the knitting was generally for somebody else—booties for a friend's baby or perhaps a scarf for one of the office boys. Aunt Alice had died in 1908, and since then the staff of the *Free Press* had become her family, though in fact anyone in need found a friend in

Cora Hind. From time to time she took in girls off the street and fed and housed them until they could find work. She had a special fund for the needy. When, after many years, she had been able to pay her bank manager the sum she had borrowed to set up her stenographer's bureau, he had refused to accept it. He knew how much she had been doing to help the Winnipeg poor, and he gave her back her loan, out of his own pocket, to use for people in distress.

After the outbreak of war in 1914, most of Cora Hind's energies went toward helping the war effort, knitting mittens and mufflers for the troops, sending comfort parcels to the office boys who had joined up and injecting a stirring brand of patriotism into her articles. To the dismay of her more pacifist friends, she supported the war wholeheartedly. Even though she was appalled by the terrible slaughter, she felt that it was the duty of all Canadians to rally to the aid of the Mother Country—and she said so loudly and often. If women had been allowed to enlist, she would have fought in the trenches herself.

Cora Hind had always been staunchly pro-British, proud of her Loyalist ancestry and proud of the fact that, by virtue of being a Canadian, she was automatically a British subject. The republicanism of the United States was not for her. Any hint of Americanization was liable to make her blood rise. One day at the *Free Press*, when the flags of various nations were being used to decorate the building for a vegetable show, she burst forth furiously when she saw that the Star-Spangled Banner had been hung above her office door.

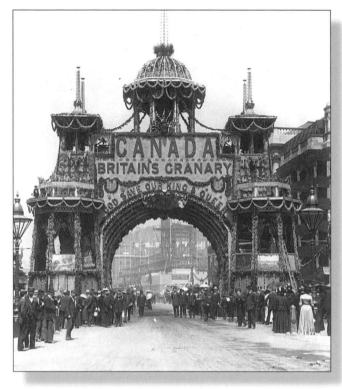

Cora Hind, like many Canadians, thought of Britain as the Mother Country

Agriculture was not the only news in Winnipeg. This famous photograph from the Winnipeg General Strike in 1919 shows the RCMP charge down Main Street.

"Take that down!" she roared—to the astonishment of the workmen who had just put it up. Ignoring the gales of laughter from her colleagues, who were thoroughly enjoying her predictable reaction, she sternly supervised while a more suitable flag was hung over the doorway.

It was also because of flags that she once reprimanded the manager of a livestock show in Chicago. Although the show was an international event with Canadian as well as American entrants, there was only one flag flying—Old Glory. Cora Hind virtually ordered the manager to add the Canadian ensign and the Union Jack. She would accept no compromise on questions of nationality.

She was, therefore, extremely annoyed when, on a visit to Great Britain after the war, she was mistaken for an American and was made to sign a special aliens' book in a hotel instead of the normal register. "I am as British as you are," she told the reception clerk indignantly. The clerk was unimpressed; no signature, no room for the night. So Cora Hind signed. But the next morning she made sure that her name was blotted out of the offensive "Register of Aliens." Still seething with outrage, she wrote a letter of protest to the *London Times*.

This incident took place in 1922, when the *Free Press* sent its agricultural editor to Britain to look into the marketing of Canadian products. It was Cora Hind's first visit to the land of her forefathers, and in a way it was a homecoming. But in fact she came not as an Englishwoman but as a Canadian. From the moment she stepped ashore, her main purpose was to promote Canadian agriculture. As it turned out, she was to do more for Canada on that one trip than all the trade commissioners and ministers of agriculture had succeeded in doing during the previous twenty years.

Working for Women – and Men

Chapter 7
Champion of Canadian Agriculture

T he famous E. Cora Hind drew considerable attention when she arrived in Britain. Officials called on her; newspapers interviewed her. Dealers, merchants and livestock breeders throughout the country were eager to meet her. She was taken on a tour of the ports so that she could see how Canadian cattle were unloaded. She was taken to Smithfield and other famous meat markets so that she could see how Canadian products were sold. She was invited to conventions, shows and banquets and was frequently asked to speak. As often as not, her speeches were then reported in the *London Times:*

> *Miss Cora Hind, agricultural editor of the* Manitoba Free Press ... *said that, speaking broadly, she had heard nothing but praise of the quality of Canadian products. There was, however, a curious thing about Canadian flour. One appeared to be unable to buy it, as such, in the retail shops. Considering the enormous quantities of Canadian flour shipped to England, this showed that Canada was missing an opportunity in some way and that it should be inquired into ... In the retail trade some funny, but irritating things were to be noted. For example, in a shop in Liverpool appeared the sign over a side of bacon, "prime Canadian bacon." The bacon was not prime, and moreover it bore the stamp of the United States. The dealer, when tackled, demanded to know what was the difference.*

As usual, E. Cora Hind was not mincing her words. And as usual, she was making sure that Canadian produce was given its due. She was one of the best advertisers the farmers ever had. When she read in the *Scottish Ayrshire Post* that a certain Mr.

Dunlop had said that the Canadian wheat crop was uncertain, she sent a furious letter to the *Post*, hotly denying his charges. Mr. Dunlop was an agricultural commissioner for Scotland who had recently visited Canada, thereby becoming an "instant expert," a veritable mine of misinformation. Among other things, he had told the *Post* readers that Canada, the land of snow, had grass for only six weeks each year. Cora Hind was not having that!

> *If grass only lasts six weeks in the year, where does Mr. Dunlop suppose Canada secured the many millions of tons of hay she exported during the war for the use, not only of her own horses and mules in France and Flanders, but for the use of Allied countries as well ...? In 1919 the province of Manitoba alone, the smallest of the three western provinces, produced $10,000,000 worth of cultivated hay.*

But Cora Hind had more to do in Britain than advertise Canadian agriculture. One of the main purposes of her trip was to get something done about the cattle embargo. Since the 1890s no Canadian cattle had been allowed into Great Britain. They had to be slaughtered on arrival at the docks. This meant that although Canadian farmers could benefit from the meat trade, they could not sell their cattle to Britain for breeding purposes or as dairy animals. Consequently, they were losing a very profitable market.

The reason for the embargo was fear of infection. Canadian cattle were said to suffer from pleuro-pneumonia, a deadly and very contagious disease. This was not in fact true. Although pleuro-pneumonia was common in the United States, Canadian cattle were disease free. They were far healthier than Irish cattle, which were allowed into Britain without any restrictions. They were among the healthiest cattle in the world. But the "American" label, which so often offended Cora Hind, had once again been extended to cover Canada. Many people in England genuinely believed that cattle from anywhere in North America might infect British herds.

Over the years the Canadian authorities had complained about the situation, and at a conference in 1917 the British had promised that the embargo would be lifted as soon as the war was over. But when Cora Hind arrived in England five years after the war, there had been no change. Canadian cattle were still suspect.

Within a few weeks of her arrival, the whole picture changed. She had, in a sense, her own broadcasting service, the many newspapers that printed her letters and reported on her activities. She made full use of them. On every possible occasion she spoke out against the embargo. She upbraided British politicians for not keeping their promise, pointing out that "the word of a British statesman will never again inspire the same blind confidence in Canada." She said that "it has been established over and over again that Canadian herds are not only healthy but they are healthier than the herds of Great Britain." She maintained that the bad reputation of Canadian cattle was wholly unjustified, and she cited evidence to prove it. As always, she could quote facts and figures from memory.

The force of her arguments had its effect. The *Times* supported her in the press; Winston Churchill supported her in the House of Commons; the Duke of Devonshire supported her in the House of Lords. A few months later, the embargo was lifted. As last, after a quarter of a century, Canada could take full advantage of the profitable British cattle market.

E. Cora Hind in 1930

E. Cora Hind was to perform a similar service on another trip to Britain in the 1930s, when Canadian dairy cows were being discriminated against. This time it was partly the fault of Canadian dealers, as she pointed out in her articles to the *Free Press*. Substandard cattle had been sent to England for breeding—old cows "with defective teeth and looking anything but attractive." Consequently, the British had started an inspection

Years of drought in the 1930s turned fertile farms into arid wastelands

system, and they had been condemning many of the cows on arrival. They were still doing so after the quality of the export cattle had been raised, because even the healthiest cows tended to be weak and sickly after a long sea voyage. This seems obvious, but it took Cora Hind to point it out and to suggest that the cattle be put out to pasture for a few weeks and then be inspected.

During these years she was also actively promoting the grain trade. With the completion of the railroad to Hudson Bay, a new and more direct route had been opened for the export of Canadian wheat. Cora Hind had long been an advocate of the Hudson Bay route, and in 1932 she sailed out of the port of Churchill—the first woman ever to do so—on board a grain ship bound for Europe. This, of course, was the best possible advertisement for the new route.

Canadian grain needed all the advertising it could get in 1932, for the Great Depression had set in and wheat had been one of the first commodities affected by the stock market crash of 1929. The price of wheat had plummeted, and the wheat pools faced a disastrous financial loss from their large unsold stocks of grain. Although the provincial governments came to the rescue with loans, the farmers were hit very hard. Some sold out and joined the unemployment lines in the cities. Others struggled on in increasingly difficult conditions, for the weather had turned against them too. Year after year there was not enough rain. The prairies became dry and dusty. Crops were poor; livestock were undernourished and thirsty. The whole agriculture of the West seemed to be crumbling to dust.

Throughout these years Cora Hind never lost her faith in the West. Although she was in her seventies by this time, she was as busy as ever, staunchly supporting all remedial programs—irrigation projects, dry-farming techniques, soil conservation, tree planting, the use of community pastures—anything and everything that might help. Meanwhile she continued to advertise Canadian products abroad and to give encouragement at home to those who were bravely trying to make a living in the dust bowl of the wind-ravaged prairies.

Her encouragement often took a personal form—perhaps spending a morning with Ukrainian homesteaders, bringing news and gifts from the outside and strengthening the family's resolve to tough it out for another year. Cora Hind had always felt a particular admiration for the non-English speakers in the West. They were isolated by their limited command of English as well as by the remoteness of their farms. She was impressed by their stoicism, the way they persevered—and succeeded—in a hostile environment.

She also appreciated the ethnic mix of Winnipeg itself, the blending of cultures that was creating a new Canada. Unfortunately, many Anglo-Saxons did not share her views. By this time Winnipeg was a large, busy city with a sizable ethnic community, and there was considerable prejudice against the Poles, the Ukrainians, the Jews—against anyone who was "different." E. Cora Hind did what she could to erase the prejudice, both by her writings and by her personal conduct. It was her custom to send a pamphlet, instead of a Christmas card, to her friends each winter. One year the pamphlet described her own neighbourhood, praising the Russian tailor, the Italian restaurateur, the Romanian fruit merchant and others. She

Cora Hind with her cat

knew that every little bit helped.

This was her attitude throughout the Depression. It was too large a problem for any one person to solve but she did what she could, giving away fifty cents here, a dollar there, though she could not always afford it. E. Cora Hind had never been rich. Even as a world-famous correspondent, she lived in a modest apartment in Winnipeg, getting by on her income with little to spare. What she did have to spare, she gave to those in need. Her generosity was so widely known that it was hard for her to enter or leave the *Free Press* building without one of the many destitute approaching her with an open hand. She always gave something, and often it was more than money. She came to know the regulars and used to stop and chat about their hometowns. "Miss Hind's boys" they were called. Most of them were in their early twenties and unable to find work. She became their friend, the first person they turned to whether they were hungry or in trouble with the police.

Cora Hind had a great many friends in all sections of the community—fellow social workers, fellow journalists, farming families that she met on her surveys, scientists that she met through her work, dairymen, cattlemen, millers, brokers, industrialists—the list is endless. Over the years they had shown their admiration in a variety of ways. In 1916 the Western Canada Livestock Union had given her a purse, containing $1300 in gold, in recognition of the work she had done for the livestock industry. In 1920 the Wool Growers of Manitoba had presented her with twenty-six young ewes. In 1927 the prestigious Canadian Society of Technical Agriculturists had made her an honorary member of their society. But the greatest honour of all came in 1935, when the University of Manitoba conferred on Cora Hind the degree of honorary doctor of law.

The day before she received her doctorate, a ceremony was held at the *Free Press* that meant as much to her, if not more, than the actual degree. In a way, it was a family affair, an expression of affection and esteem from those nearest and dearest to her. Gathering the staff together, Dafoe formally presented Cora Hind with the gown to wear at her graduation, telling her:

John W. Dafoe reads a speech of congratulations to Cora Hind on the granting of her honorary doctor of law degree from the University of Manitoba

Honorary degrees of the University of Manitoba are conferred in very limited numbers, on persons falling within two categories, those who have rendered outstanding public service and those who have achieved outstanding academic distinction ... As a specialist and authority in your particular field, you have built a reputation which is world wide; and you could go nowhere where agricultural pursuits are intelligently followed that you would not find yours a known and familiar name.

He concluded his speech in a more person vein, expressing the staff's great regard for her, their pride in her achievements and their good wishes for her future.

In reply Cora Hind could do little more than say thank-you. For once in her life, she was at a loss for words. "You are my family," she murmured," and I am very, very grateful." However, she was completely in control of her emotions when, the following day, wearing the scarlet academic gown, she walked proudly beside the dean of the university in the procession towards the convocation hall.

When she left the hall, she was Dr. E. Cora Hind.

Chapter 8
Friend, Specialist, Great Canadian

ora Hind was seventy-four years old when she received her doctorate, but she was not ready to retire. In 1935 she set off around the world on a roving commission for the *Free Press*, sending the paper articles on places as far afield as Australia, South America, Europe and India. In every country her investigations were as thorough as ever. Indeed, the reports she sent back were so much to the point—and so popular—that a selection of them was published as a book called *Seeing for Myself*.

After two years of seeing for herself, Dr. Hind returned to Winnipeg, ready to go back to work. But Dafoe had thought of the world trip as a kind of retirement gift, a farewell present to crown a long and distinguished career. Tactfully, he suggested that running a busy department might be too much to ask of her at the age of seventy-six. So she agreed to give up her position as agricultural and commercial editor. But she did not retire. She joined the paper's general writing staff and continued to make the rounds of cattle shows and conventions and, of course, to send in articles. When in 1942, at the age of eighty-one, her health finally failed, she was halfway through an article. Typically, she was

E. Cora Hind inspecting grain

E. Cora Hind late in life. When she died, trading was suspended for two minutes at the Winnipeg Grain Exchange.

also halfway through a piece of knitting—a khaki sock destined for one of the soldiers fighting in World War II.

She had been suffering from heart trouble for some years, and then in September 1942 a blood clot blocked the artery of her left arm. She refused to have her arm in a sling and would not take to her bed. But she did agree to employ a full-time nurse, though who was caring for whom is difficult to judge. One day in October, seeing that the nurse looked tired, Dr. Hind suggested a walk round the block to get some air. "I'll be all right here for a while," she assured the nurse cheerfully. But she was not all right. She began to feel desperately ill shortly after the nurse had gone out. Struggling to her feet, she made her way across the hall to a friend's apartment. "I think I'm dying," she announced calmly. "Would you ask the nurse to hurry?" Soon after this she suffered a stroke, from which she never regained consciousness. She died the following day, October 6, 1942.

And so at last the dean of Canadian newspaperwomen did retire from her work—and from life. Right across the world there was a sense of shock. E. Cora Hind was a Canadian institution; it was hard to think of western agriculture without her. The people of Winnipeg took her death as a personal loss, and many felt compelled to express their sorrow in letters to the *Free Press*. They spoke especially of Dr. Hind's kindness. They recalled the work she had done for the people of the city through the WCTU and other organizations. They praised her as friend and neighbour, as author and journalist. Others wrote of her energy and ability, her crop reports, her service to the various branches of agriculture. They recalled how, during her long life, she had seen the West develop beyond belief and how she had contributed to that development. Friend, writer, specialist, pioneer, great Canadian—Dr. E. Cora Hind was remembered in all these roles. Yet perhaps none of the tributes expressed her distinction as well as the *Calgary Albertan* had done some years earlier:

> *The pages of western history are bright with the names of many great women—women who have become great by their heroism, by their devotion, by their saintliness; but Cora Hind is a great woman in a way different from all these. In a day when woman's place was the home and even the most emancipated might never think of more liberty than the schoolroom, Miss Hind was bold enough to shoulder her way into the ranks of men, and she has been shouldering among them ever since, as the equal of any of them and as the superior of most.*

This was surely E. Cora Hind's greatest achievement. Her entire life can be seen as a statement of ability—of a woman's ability to excel in what was considered a man's world. As she once remarked, "When the last word is said, women are the race, and it is their thought and their work and their actions which will mould the future race as they have in the past."

E. Cora Hind

1861	Ella Cora Hind is born in Toronto on September 18
1882	Writes her third-class teacher's examination and fails; moves to Winnipeg with her Aunt Alice
1883	Gets job as a "type-writer" with lawyers Macdonald and Tupper; joins WCTU
1893	Starts first public stenographer's bureau in the West
1895	Becomes western correspondent for Maclean's Publications
1898	Makes first crop prediction for Maclean's
1901	Appointed to staff of *Manitoba Free Press*
1904	Makes second crop prediction when rust epidemic hits prairies
1903	Helps form the Quill Club, an informal literary group
1908	Aunt Alice dies
1912	Helps form the Political Equality League for women's suffrage
1913	Criticized for making low, but accurate, crop prediction
1914	Takes part in a Mock Parliament with other suffragettes
1916	Receives $1300 as tribute from Western Canada Livestock Union
	Manitoba grants women the right to vote in provincial elections
	Manitoba Temperance Act bans sale of liquor in the province
1920	Presented with 26 ewes by Wool Growers of Manitoba
1922	Travels to Britain for *Free Press* to investigate marketing of Canadian products
1927	Made honorary member of Canadian Society of Technical Agriculturists
1932	Sails from Churchill on a grain ship bound for Europe
1935	Receives honorary doctorate from University of Manitoba
	Travels around the world on a roving commission for the *Free Press*
1942	Dies on October 6, following a stroke

Sincerely yours

L Chatfield

Gauvin Gentzel Co
Winnipeg

Further Reading

Benham, Mary Lile. *Nellie McClung*, Don Mills, Ont.: Fitzhenry & Whiteside, 1975.

Collins, Paul. *Hart Massey*, Don Mills, Ont.: Fitzhenry & Whiteside, 1978.

Gray, James H. *Booze*, Toronto: Macmillan of Canada, 1972.

Haig, Kennethe. *Brave Harvest*, Toronto: Thomas Allen, 1945.

Haig, Kennethe. *"E.Cora Hind" in The Clear Spirit*, edited by Mary Quayle Innis, Toronto: University of Toronto Press, 1966.

Hind, E. Cora. *Seeing for Myself.* Toronto: Macmillan of Canada, 1937.

Mason, Helen. *Settlement of the West: Cora Hind, journalist.* Grolier Limited, c1990

McClung, Nellie. *The Stream Runs Fast*, Toronto: Thomas Allen, 1945.

Neering, Rosemary. *Settlement of the West*, Don Mills Ont.: Fitzhenry & Whiteside, 1974.

Pomeroy, Elsie M. *William Saunders and His Five Sons: The Story of the Marquis Wheat Family*, Toronto: Ryerson, 1956.

Credits

The publishers wish to express their thanks to the following for their kind assistance during the preparation of this book: Mrs. Leslie N. Hall, who was for many years E. Cora Hind's secretary; the staff of the *Winnipeg Free Press;* the staff of the Provincial Archives of Manitoba; and Mrs. Helena Haberman of Winnipeg.

The publishers are grateful to Thomas Allen and Sons of Toronto and to the Provincial Archives of Manitoba for permission to quote copyright material and to the following who have given permission to use copyrighted illustrations in this book:
Alberta Archives, Glenbow Institute, pages 21(NA-3199-1), 53(NA-1451-10)
Canada Archives, pages 25(PA-027942), 29(PA-031489), 34(PA-021460), 35(C-008893), 41(PA-118067), 45(C-033509), 49(C-063260), 50(C-037275)
Manitoba Archives, pages 11, 14, 19, 20, 24, 25, 26, 33, 38, 44, 46, 47, 54, 59
Ontario Archives, pages 8(S13674), 9(S627)
Toronto Public Library, pages 17, 18, 22, 60, 63(Thomas Allen Collection)
Winnipeg Free Press, pages 3, 5, 56, 57
Every effort has been made to credit all sources correctly. The publishers will welcome any information that will allow them to correct any errors or omissions.

Index